Asylum

Asylum

and Other Poems

JERRY PINTO

SPEAKING
TIGER

SPEAKING TIGER BOOKS LLP
4381/4, Ansari Road, Daryaganj
New Delhi 110002

First published by Allied Publishers 2003
This revised edition published by Speaking Tiger Books 2021

ISBN: 978-93-90477-68-5
eISBN: 978-93-90477-70-8

10 9 8 7 6 5 4 3 2 1

Typeset in EB Garamond by SÜRYA, New Delhi
Printed at Chaman Enterprises, New Delhi

To my father Augustine,
my mother Imelda and my sister Andrea.

CONTENTS

Prayer

Lord of the linear narrative,
Show me the point at which I should begin.
Stop me when I have said as much as I should.
Regulate my voice, I boom too much
and my whispers are shrill.
Feed me words on those long, slow afternoons.
Allow me the grace of serendipity—
To find lost continents on my tongue.
Give me the gift of silence,
and then set me adrift.

Asylum

Chemical soup stilled,
It is a harsh harbour we have found for you.
Becalmed, you loll at anchor.
Barnacles cling to you; their slime-scented kisses
Send rot shivering through your timbers.
Your nails are copper-tinted, varnished, unchipped
And your holds filled with pebbles, lacquered pink,
A ballast of torpor.

Beyond the headlands lie the unsuspected fires
Of alien mornings flecked red with maritime superstition.
Our eyes ache with watchfulness;
Sleep is inevitable and the slippage
Of anchor, and sense and what love means.

When the sky screams, the blowtorch is wise.
In the calm, the encrusted stains, blood, rust,
Mock those decisions. What watches us?
Those holes we cut to still you, are those your eyes?

The Quiet Rebellion of Paper

See here on this maculate page
A poem struggled for breath
Spat black blood and died.

And here, on this one,
A letter left its nail marks
As it lost its hold and fell into the abyss.

See this hard-edged invitation
Serrated in two for memoranda
With stillborn plans born one optimistic morning.

Paper is the measure and metaphor of our lives;
Our order's young faith rests
In white corpseflakes that burn well,
Tear easily, crumple eagerly, fade gracelessly
And cannot resist the blandishments of water.

Paper is order and method, we think.
But on a hot neap-tide night
Paper will rebel
Quietly.

Discarded drafts will invade files
Shredded printouts will heal along the seams
Chaperoned incunabula will mate with pocket books
Illuminated manuscripts will break from the vaults
And head to the fire in kamikaze squads.

And we?
What of us, then?
Oh but it is a sultry night
And we are sleeping.
Our mouths hang open, stitched to the pillows
With fine threads of saliva.
Runnels of sweat course through our hair
and each breath is foetid with floss.

We will rise coughing in the dawn
To a new world:
Rivers black with ink
Bank notes printed with runes
Textbooks in lost languages
Poetry replaced by *Reader's Digest* mailers,
And we will deserve it too.

Exiled Home from Burma

I

'We must leave behind
The coal mine and the teak plantation
The trays of sweets sent by debtors
And the memory of morning massages,'
Said my grandmother. Her ears,
Preternaturally sharp, could hear
Hitler goose-stepping (by proxy)
Through melted forests of teak.

II

'By all the laws of navigation, ma'am
A lighter ship may travel faster,'
Said the captain and went hunting.
He found a piano; a mastodon mired
In Mozart, it was trapped quickly
And drowned well.
Once the Shwe Dagon ignored
Scales played by dutiful fingers.
Now fan-tailed fish lodge in its shell.

III

'Bombs have no eyes.
They will not see it is my Johnny,
A good boy who took his mother dancing.
But God has ears that we can storm
And my Johnny has strong legs,'
Said my great-grandmother,
Her brood gathered around her.

IV

Orange sweets may fail you
Melting glutinously in fat-necked bottles;
Orange peel will not.
Dry, it will dispel the nausea of exile;
Wet, it will spurt rage into the eyes
Of a wet-lipped sailor
Attracted by the smell of a girl's first bleeding.

Cetacean Song

Bound by the need for breath
We lie on beds of foaming rubber.
But the room is filled with
The rhythm of blood and need and the story.

We lie quietly, listening.
The whales are singing each to each.
It is my last article of belief:
They understand their music.
You and I only have words.

Outside the window
The sea, the sea.

At Thirty

I thought I would grow used to this body.
Thirty years together and we've had it easier than some
(Discount a fracture or two, minus some teeth).
We should have struck a balance now;
Three decades is enough time to reconcile
The myopia and the clumsiness,
The hair receding where it ought to grow,
Sprouting cheerfully where it ought not.
I should be able to live in here now.

Now they tell me this is a new body:
Every cell is different, except for the brain.
All the old cells gone, sloughed off,
Recycled, born again.
So now I know why this body is a stranger
Unfamiliar in sudden mirrors,
Alien in old photographs.

And I know that another body awaits me
And another, another.
Each rebellious, each different, uncompromising,
Each with built-in state-of-the-art aches.

New each time, each pang new.
My body in name only
My body that refuses to settle down
My body that will not acknowledge me.

'Well, If You're a Poet, Write Me a Poem.'

I thought about it
I thought about it and decided
That for you it must be another kind of poem;
A seed poem.

You can do so much with a seed poem.
Plant it, nurture it, breathe on it
So that one day it burgeons,
Brings forth ripe, unsegmented fruit.

But seed poems need much more than good intentions.
We stuck ours into a pot, a bonsai pot
With glass bits cut into its sides.
With nail scissors, we snipped its leaves,
Forced it to fruit and closed our ears
To its green screams.

So this time I thought about it:
I'm going to give you a deodorant.
Be careful: its contents are inflammable
And stored under pressure.

Dadiba's Matka

As Dadiba shrivelled and died
His matka began to bloom
Until the roaches walked from it
Coated with pollen.
Moss festooned it without and within.
It was alluvial with silt so rich
It grew orchids.
(If you looked into one long enough
And then at a white wall,
You'd see Dadiba's face
Or so it was whispered.)

By its side sat a dipper
With a dent in it
The precise shape of the depression
Between Dadiba's skull and collar.
When he was thirsty, Dadiba sounded his matka
With the dipper
And listened carefully
To its deep belling note.
Only when it had slaked his ears
Would he drink.

What did Dadiba hear?
For thirty years, he cohabited with that matka,
Defended it from his mother's steelwool hands.
When she cross-stitched the air with a motto—
'Cleanliness is next to Godliness,'—
Dadiba retorted,
'Let's be godly instead.'

Then Dadiba died and we looked at his matka.
We hoped it would change, show some remorse
for its obscene succulence; crack perhaps,
Spilling a new helix.
Or even just bay at the moon.

It did nothing.

Now you know why we planted a mango in it
And cried out with horror
When its root cracked
Dadiba's matka.

For Allan, Whom I Never Saw

A blue bead glinted in a dark room
And drew your starfish hand.
You sent it out to explore
The drumlin of a familiar sofa.

Only a baby could be distracted
From the important business of dying.

You are going to die tonight, Allan.
That walk in the dew was fatal.
But your lungs spare you pain;
They close down quietly.

You lie limp on your grandmother's lap
As they run for a doctor, rouse a car.
You rattle, wheeze, die.
They limp to the undertaker.

In the next room, your mother sleeps.
You reach out a starfish hand
Eager to be lifted by the tide.

Rain

This is the building built on the lot
That once stood for my desert.
When my head could get through
The grills of the gate,
This lot was large and desolate;
Its redness defeating all but the strong.

The rain was not meant to come through.
The walls were not meant to turn green.
I tried to build a new moss world,
Where rivers would incise forests
And leaf mould would clot the cream
Of the school building's walls.

A nocturnal hand felled the forest.
It was used to the symmetry of grave stones
And to the incorruptible nature of nylon socks.
Walled-in, the earth dried.
The forests clumped away.
I lost interest in maps.

Outside, the slate skies crumbled.
Grit scoured the wet streets
And the air was grey, infected silk:
Smooth, soft, old,
A powdery cheek at a funeral.

Old Wall

Somewhere I see an old wall:
Home to a thousand self-contained ecosystems,
A chiaroscuro of moss and crumbling stone
Beneath a parade of triumphant strutting leaves.
Hard as wood, roots coil into nooses,
Deliberately strangling its stones.
The wall has not been abandoned:
It bears fresh weals of lovers' promises.

Last week, we liberated some wallspores,
Transplanted them into the new soil
Of a fallow beginning.
And so do walls
Perpetuate themselves.

Incident at Chira Bazaar

We walked along the road running river
But the current was too strong.
All around there were people like us
Nice people whose niceness flashed at us
Like dark dorsal fins rising out of the foam.
A creek appeared, sluggish backwater
That promised the sedation of tea.

We found it, skewered to a wall
By faith and lampblack. Across from it
There was a shrine and a bench;
The saint, benign, an ankle resting on a knee,
Offered his roof to everyone
And would not refuse it to outcasts like us,
Drenched in respectability and shivering.

You opened the packet of farsan.
I groped in my bag of conversation.
But it was the drunkard who found names for us:
Baby and Raju.
He had had too much today, Raju, and he knew it.
Lost his bag, his slippers, his foothold in the river.

He has a room and four children, Raju.
If I meet him tomorrow, he'll show me.
'Only today, Raju today is different.'
He is not after my wife, Raju
He has his own.
'Ay, Baby, Ay!'
His voice rises.

The community of the chillum is hospitable
Laidback and willing to pass it twice more.
They are slow but they know what they are about,
There are uncertain hierarchies here on the margin.
The community of the chillum is hospitable.
They rise to prove it
They welcome us by slapping the man
Stand him up, slap him again, again.
They are slow, chimney-smoke on a winter morning,
But fast enough for him.
One push will do it.
One push does it.

The man falls
Strikes his head on the tea stall.
Freeze frame for blood.
Nothing.
He lies there dazed, waiting:
Still no blood.

The community coagulates again
Blue gauze veils descend on them.
The man folds his body; abases his forehead
Weeps softly, and wails.

We finish our tea, abandon our farsan
To well-fed puppies, tan and black.
They are plump with trust
And the stale bread from the first floor.

The veil parts to receive our thanks
Good guests must thank the hospitable,
Leave boons or privileges,
Submerge a village
Or punish a man.
How else will we learn to see
God in every footsore beggar?

We plunge towards the welcoming river
Where people glide past, streamlined.
We avoid each other's eyes
And then I catch a glint of my knife
In your rust-flecked armour
And I say,
'He started it.'

For My Students

'How like that, Jerry?'
You ask and I struggle for an answer.
The logic of catechisms will not work here,
Nor the sanities of experimental psychology.
To answer you, I must bare myself,
Show you the bedsores on my self,
Tell you how I have wanted to ask the same questions,
Tell you how I have accepted the same lies.

Ask me to explain calculus instead;
I can handle that.
But when you drop your turgid animal hearts
into my hands, beware,
My frosted fingers
May leave ice burn.

So I say, 'That could be phrased better, you know.'

This Summer

This summer
It wasn't the seismic nature of heat,
Not just the rivulets of sweat encrusting my skin
Nor the Martian mud lifted by thirsty park winds.

This summer
It wasn't supposed to be love.
There was feeling of a kind
And at least one night of pure romance.

This summer
It wasn't me. Or you:
It was the sugary, lard-rich meals
We fed each other.
We called it sensual,
Scooping calcium-enriched, hot-pink royal jelly
From hexagonal, porcelain pots.

We fattened on it.
We watched each other bloat
In mirrors
Because we could not meet each other's eyes.

When it was over and we had
Shed kilos, burnt letters,
Dismantled structures of deception,
Tried to forgive ourselves,
We met again.
And only then
We called it love.

Sleep

I

On this dead red plateau, there are stones, which crack to reveal a treasury of facets, avidly reflecting the jaundiced light of the afternoon, rinsing themselves of the memory of darkness, centuries of darkness.

Some stones. Only some stones.

You squat,

You creak from patch to patch,

And very often you must have recourse to the little stall near the bus-stand where they sell these stones with smirks of understanding and bottles of cold soda.

II

The night bears on and with a troubled sigh she tries to turn over. You reach out and straighten the pillow, worry at the mattress. You know the rules and the reasons. She must not turn because of the drip. She must stay in position and you must keep her there.

You wonder whether she needs something.
Water?
A sedative?
Reassurance?

You cannot fathom that need. Or that moment when the eyes really closed, denying you the faint slivers of white striated with grey-black lashes. Or that smile, quick, hesitant, a baby's smile of foetal memory. You cannot fathom the whispers and the sighs, the threshing of a veined hand, the deeply etched frown.

Does she remember the girl of eighteen who went with her brother's disembodied arm around her shoulders to Burma, to Jocasta, and the forbidden gleam of golden pagodas?

Does she remember the son whose curly head nuzzled her body drinking milk and blood and pus from the abscess on her breast?

Does she remember the first grey rebellion of her lungs, the first blood-black effusions from her gut?

Does she remember the cloth bags? The cut-work pillow cases of Mother Martha? The nuns and their unending unwashed floors?

Does she remember the boy who sent her a tray of creams, beguiled by her loveliness?

Does she remember how death hovered around her twice before?

Or is she here, in the present, in the hushed dawning?

III

When morning comes, she wakes and sees and smiles in recognition. Her voice is a thread of rusty sound asking for tea. She has forgotten the night and what it brought.

You are at the bus-stand together.

Rictus

The men who came to dress his body
Laid tender hands on his face.
Their first job, they knew, was to erase
That rictus of shock.

Death has a grim sense of humour.
One Saturday night, it tapped him
On the shoulder, handed him a toy.
Puzzled, he took it, shook it.
He rattled.

That dark red tub, my uncle's, has seen many uses.
It can tell you stories, mundane ones
And some perverse bloody horrors.
You will not wash him with detergent?
You will.

Mummy is in the next room.
I watch her between tasks. She does not react.
Mention coffins and her golden eyes do not flinch.
Buy rock salt and she asks: 'Why rock salt?'
'To absorb what flows out of the body.'

What flows out of his body?
Ordinary dreams and old fables.
A few riddles, a moral or two, some gaps.
The last, fear.

'Wait a whole night,' he told us,
'Before you bury me.' We did.
Was there something else, Daddy,
Some other instruction?
Something we forgot?

Letter

(For Arundhathi)

What chance does a letter have of getting written?
Exoneration comes in different guises:
Circles, lies, lines, lacunae, Mobius strips.

What chance does a letter have?
The imbalance is here.
Pen touches paper
And the hopeless underbelly of longing is exposed,
So pleasing elsewhere, so leprous in the mirror.
An aching wrist, empty ears are not enough.
What chance does a letter have?

Everything here seems larger than it.
The whitewash on the walls laughs at the forlorn option.
Those hands are calloused;
The descent of the stamp on the vulnerable surface.
The queen apologises for stepping on the hangman's toes.

What chance does a letter have?
Overwhelmed by a semi-circular sky and a diametric sea,
Weighing at so many grammes and so many rupees
Against millions of tonnes of air and parody.

What chance does it have?
The demand for reciprocity denies anyone satisfaction.
It is twice cursed; it curses both ends of the chain,
The middle rejoices on festivals.

What chance has it? Acid digests its fibres as use has
corroded its tropes—
The tear-stain, the lipstick smear, the purple ribbon.

What chance
Against its own words?

Dreaming at Mukesh Mills

He walked under the trees right up to the gates,
Defending his head from vengeful monkeys.
July and the rain came down in rapiers;
The sea drank, but only vintage plasma
Then the first whistle woke the machines
Sent spires of smoke to mate grey with grey.

Between the thump of bales and the scratch of pen
He had room for an errant empire of the mind.
He saw heaps of pearls at Aden Custom House
And the sun-warmed salt of a sweaty rebellion.
Whoever designed this space knew
That clerks, like poets, need to dream.

Then his son came there to balance on a rafter.
He singed a cellophane future with cold white light
In this new-rendered space, he could have no dreams.
The lash of waves was ambient noise to him.
He could not hear the sea's blood-sated purr
As he walked high in the fretted skull of its kill.

Mid-afternoon. One day, he comes back to the mill
For the dreary business of a lost cause.
The hoarse voices around him become tug-boat cries,
The sun is a floodlight, he is reeled up flat.
The mill will go. The sun will lose.
He can taste defeat and it is strangely like his own spit.

Alphabet Soup

A is alone
and afraid of responsibility.
A is fragile
Two sticks holding a third in place.

X marks the spot
Failure lies buried here.
X is a stranger
Sand-pitted from the winds
That blew outside Khwarizmi's tent.

Y is a cleft stick, dangerous.
Y can hurt
When aimed at smudge of
Down and wing;
And the things we do.

i
is
that a halo? Or a birthmark?

Q after Q after q after q, after, after.

If B is pregnant with meaning
R has given birth.
To a Snake.

On Swallowing the Pit of a Peach

The fecund promise of fruit lures me.
Under the white dust of fat-soluble death:
A maroon glow, wet flesh, obscenely pitted seed.
I swallow the wizened brain of Satan.
Through the night I will be
The soil in which he takes root,
Coils around my spine.

My mouth is susurrant with leaves.
My sternum turns to wood.
I am alive with sap
And the mineral promise of water.
I am alive to the staccato music
Of hoof and tail.
But I will be dead when you play on me.

Some Questions I Want Answered

We never had time to talk
And then I would not have known
What I wanted to ask.
Forgive me, ex-Significant Other,
And let me ask now.

My mother said she felt a click
When the sun inside her melted
To laughter and life at the sight
Of that writhing, relentless
Comic-come-courting.
Did you?

That wave-drenched suddenness
Is with me still. I walk there crunching
Perfect shells, dislodging crabs.
Do you walk with me?

The missed harvest of snow hibiscus and pain,
The lonely moment of ceramic-tiled fear,
The mockery of diced papaya, wrought with lemon and honey.
Would it have been easier if you had shared it?

The second, split by decision.
The servant-girl's shades.
Your oiled hair.
The taxi.
And then another, doubling back.
The manoeuvres, the moves, the deceits
I would they were mine.
Do you believe me?

I can't remember what I said
But I remember your red nails flashing,
Your teeth clamped in my wrist.
Those moments, fevered, urgent, breathless.
So much like love, this final rage.
What did I say?

And this, I promise, will be the last.
Do you live in terror of a chance meeting,
A semaphored recognition, a face jerked away?
For all these questions, I'll answer this one:
I do.

Pigeon

I

When I asked what iridescent meant
My mother said, 'Like pigeon necks.'
I thought there were no male pigeons.
I thought male pigeons were crows.

II

When Andrea was born
When her eyes turned green
They were the colour of pigeon necks.
The pigeons came to roost
Around her cradle.

III

The boys came for the pigeons
In a pincer motion.
(White teeth at the door
Black hair at the window box.)
The pigeons only flap harshly;
They know the futility
Of cries for help.
Last clear memory?
A bird resting in a hand.

IV

The eggs were small
White, perfect, as large as rubies.
After he threw stones at them
They turned yellow.
Ants cleared the debris.
And finally, finally you could lean
Over the balcony
Head almost in the box
And not smell their acrid odour.

V

For a moment they are scales
Then fungus infesting a tree
Or promising the stench of fruit.
Then the angel passes
And the pigeons
Become birds again.

Desk Clearance

All afternoon, I have tried to clean this space.
No easy task, it calls for a harsh dominion,
A fierce exercise of will. Each paper is a palimpsest,
All the oddments seem worthy of redemption.

I begin quietly, ripping up evidence,
But a fury builds, my hands become fire.
I scorch through the undergrowth
Flushing out the furry mammals of old ambitions.

Yes, Emily, now a formal feeling comes.
I understand the extended self; it was here
Sprawled over this table, doppelganger of my mind.
It is here now: flat, brown, coffee-scarred.

4 A.M.

Because I was not warned
I ate more than a pomegranate.
Now, sated, I have no bones
To pass between the bars.

I was not warned
And so, I helped no old ladies,
Saved no ants,
Arrived with no bread.

I rise early
I watch the beast.
Its muzzle points out to sea
Its hot breath fans the waves
Its hairless breast heaves
Collapses, heaves.

Its power is enormous.
When it awakes, it can vanish,
Inducing dreams of lotus-eating
And autonomy.

But it is there
And it looks into the same mirrors.
It eats the same garlic.
It scratches its back on the crosses:
The city.

Security

At eight,
the backseat of a car
can be a cocoon
spun from the drifting threads
of parents talking in the front seat.
You float there
in warm-scented space
and rest your cheek
against the metallic amnion
of the car.

Do not sleep, child, do not sleep,
Just drowse along, enjoy the floating.
One day you will inherit the front seat.

Do not think of that either.
For then the road lurches
and branches reach talons
through the window.
Sleek forms with delirious eyes
run alongside, wheedling
the wheel from you.

The fibres are now corrosive:
angry voices rising;
cocoon tearing, now a
cell of helplessness.
Perhaps it is best to sleep now.

Tree 1

In a churchyard
A mango tree dies.
Militant creeper with leaves
As large as choristers' faces
Digs gentle tendrils into a bark
That should have known better.
The tree murmurs in the sunshine
Hangs out dull bulbs of sour green
In anticipation of its funeral.

Tree 2

When you plant a graveyard favourite
In a window-box, you should not blame it later.
Vinca, perennial vinca,
Killed the fern, aborted the rose
Ravaged the nameless burst of red flowers
We brought home from Seminary Hill.
Vinca: pink or white, five-petalled
And inevitable
Like death.

Tree 3

Some trees understand their contract with the city.
Not the banyan.
Misunderstanding is heavy and finally the banyan tilts,
The city props it up.
It seems a shame to plant a banyan in the city.

Tree 4

You are not a baobab.
You are a complacent, middle-class
Clerk-in-a-sari
Who would not share her chestnuts.

Tree 5

Like that assassin, love,
the streetlight waited quiescent
within your leaves;
waited for night, waited for rain
and struck.

How brightly you burn, tree:
Like your yellow flowers with
their dark red violent hearts.

Tree 6

Not so much a tree-trunk
As a gush of melting wood:
The mane of Medusa after an oiling
Dripping cannon-balls of seed-rich sweat.

From Another Planet

Topography

The black sun is ruled by tides
That run through her anarchic estuaries.
No one has studied them yet;
For the tides rule the sun
And the sun rules them all.

Flora and Fauna

Two ceramic leaves
One smashed, the other in hiding.
Two armour-plated fish
Who eat enough to stay alive
And pay blank-eyed homage to
The sun.
(See also History)

History

The only events are fruit-flies
That skim the surface-tension of the tides.

Weather

First the sun is a foetus,
Timid in a threatening sky.
The fish snap at events,
Savour their evanescence.

Then the tides begin to rage again.
The sea swallows the sun.
Refracted, the sun turns red.
The fish exhale, plumes of rocksalt.
The waters froth.
Everywhere they turn, there is
The Sun.

Mythology

This is what the fish believe:
'There are other planets
Uninfected by paradox;
We can go there
Some day.'

Present Status

Quo

Bedside

I watch your face hanging open
Your warm wet mouth, your tongue flickering
Your spectacles grimy, your hair alive
Your forehead broad and wasted
Your cheeks alternately limp and bulging.

I do not need to watch your body
I have tended it often
Eased its pains with capsicum plasters
And prayed I was easing your mind too
With my litany fresh off the shelf:
Tegretol, Anxol, Espazine, Hexidol
Neurobion, Arrovit, Shelcal, Diazepam.
I cross your palm with powder
And pray that you should not
Tell my future.

When I last lifted you off the floor
You were sitting close to my bed.
You did not expect to fall
Not under the knowing eyes of
Mother of Perpetual Succour.
I direct your gaze to the falling slipper

Of the child in her arms.
It falls, you told me some lives ago
Out of fear of the foretold future
I understand that slippage.
But you? You live it.

Some nights you let me sleep in patches.
I have grown used to it, relying on my
Ability to turn you off, and your pain.
I have survived to write these lines
To turn you, baste you and marinate
Our twinned lives into a poem.
But I wish I could keep
My heart unguilty, my love fresh
My thoughts wide-ranging, my eyes new
And that wound—inflicted on days of empathy—
Raw and open.

There are many options I know:
The glaze of stillness and the panacea of forgetfulness
Or the black snot that stained granny's kerchief;
A trust in the occult, born of grief;
A faith in God, born of habit.
So many options and I, on auto-pilot,
Cross your palm with powder.

Outside, I turn my face to the sun
Laugh, play, pun, work, entertain, function.
I know from a few grim examples
And one bright shining one
How the world fêtes facades;
I have grown used to seeing the one I devised
Reflected in your laughter-silted eyes.

Inside, I shrink from metaphor and magic.
I have no beliefs here, only a watchfulness.
My world condenses into an ink-stain
As your voice trails after me from room to room.
I made promises for you, standing in the toilet
By the skull of the Cyclops that drank my piss.
I broke those promises, one by one
And know that is why I cannot love.

Mummy, find it in you to forgive me
And I will try to be bigger than my guilt
And forgive myself.

Acknowledgements

Some of these poems appeared in *The Indian PEN, The Economic Times, The Independent, Debonair, The Brown Critique, Poesis* and *The Little Magazine*. Thanks are due to the editors of all these magazines.

Four of the poems were collected in *Reasons for Belonging* (Penguin India; 2001) edited by Ranjit Hoskote.

I would also like to thank all the members of the Poetry Circle, Bombay; fellow-pilgrims.

ALSO FROM SPEAKING TIGER

I WANT A POEM

and other poems

Jerry Pinto

I want a poem like an animal.
You should be able to eat it. Or domesticate it.
You should be able to befriend it. Or behead it.
You could carry it around or make it bear your burdens.
You could, should, oh should, so should, clean up after it.

Wondering poems, wise poems. Fierce poems and playful poems. Poems about everyday things and uncommon things. Poems of isolation and fellowship; about loving and leaving, finding and losing and finding again.

Jerry Pinto's second collection of poetry sparkles and soothes; in words that always ring true, it shows us what it means to be human, and how to be human. In his verse, as in his prose, Pinto is a writer to come home to.